LET GO OF THE SH*! SHOW WORKBOOK

{ Conquer Your **"SUCCESSFUL DISCONTENT"** *and* Live Free and Fulfilled }

MICHAEL R. VUKELIC

Let Go of the Shit Show WORKBOOK
Conquer Your "Successful Discontent" And Live Free And Fulfilled

© 2020 Michael Vukelic. All rights reserved.

Printed in the United States of America. No part of this book may be used or Reproduced in any manner whatsoever without written permission except in the case of brief quotations embodied in critical articles and review.

Edited by: Danne Reed
Cover Designed by: Kendra Cagle
Book Interior Designed by: Kendra Cagle

ISBN: 978-0-578-71093-8

Additional books by Michael Vukelic may be purchased at:
OutrageousSuccess.com

Outrageous Success
400 Washington Street
Northfield, MN 55057

{ INTRODUCTION }

✱ ✱ ✱

THIS WORKBOOK IS MEANT TO BE USED AS A COMPANION TO THE BOOK OF THE SAME TITLE:

Let Go of The Shit Show:
Conquer Your "Successful Discontent" and Live Free and Fulfilled

Inside the pages of this workbook lies a new you. An aware, awakened you. The questions and processes contained within are designed to be uplifting and engaging and follow the content and flow of the original book. The workbook is intended to be a fun discovery process and bring new meaning to your adventure of life. Allow yourself to have fun with it. As you uncover new knowledge may you find empowerment, joy and a profound new love of self. Enjoy!

For more information visit: Letgotheshitshow.com.

QUANTUM LEAP
SUCCESS PROGRAM

COMING HOME

PERSONAL I.

Authentic
Courageous
Confident
Powerful
Free

Beliefs
Personal Truth
Social Mask
Stories
Patterns

LOVE

Intention
Service
Relationship
Abundance
Health

Universal Fears
Forgiveness
Value
Trust
Acceptance

END RESULT

LOVE THYSELF

© 2020 Michael Vukelic. All rights reserved.

CHAPTER 1

***

LIFE *is* WONDERFUL...
and then IT ISN'T

1. Identify what you really love about your life. What people, places or events make you happy? And Why? What is it about your day that feels good?

   _____
   _____
   _____
   _____

2. Take a look at a typical day in your life. What stories do you tell yourself? Is there a recurring pattern of thought that you return to that leaves you upset, dissatisfied, discontent or discouraged?

   _____
   _____
   _____
   _____

3. How often do you return to feeling this way?

   _____
   _____
   _____
   _____

4. Identify, who or what you blame in your life for situations, conversations or events that upset you or leave you feeling mediocre.

   _____
   _____
   _____
   _____

5. How well do you understand your needs and desires and (with out comparing yourself to others,) how would you rate your overall connection with those desires?

   _____
   _____
   _____
   _____

6. Considering your relationships, love, career, abundance, and health, on a scale of 1 - 10, how fulfilled are you with these ares of your life?

   _____
   _____
   _____

7. What one thing do you really want to change? How committed are you to changing this?

   _____
   _____
   _____

{ CHAPTER 2 }

***

The SUCCESSFUL LIFE

1. *If you could change anything in your life, right now, what would you change? Be specific. List the changes you desire.*

   _____
   _____
   _____
   _____

2. *What does your "successful" life look like today? Upon making all the changes you desire, what would your life look like then?*

   _____
   _____
   _____
   _____

3. *What dims your light? Can you identify what you are settling for in specific areas of life? Work or Career? Love or relationship?*

   _____
   _____
   _____
   _____

4. *Do you compare your life to others? How do you see yourself? What happens when you do?*

   _____
   _____
   _____
   _____

5. *Are you concerned about what others think? Why?*

   _____
   _____
   _____
   _____

6. *What fears are present when you consider changing your life? What do you worry about most?*

   _____
   _____
   _____
   _____

7. *What are you getting out of staying in your current situation? What is the benefit and why do you stay?*

   _____
   _____
   _____
   _____

{ **CHAPTER 3** }

* * *

The BEGINNINGS

1. *Take as much time as you need and write your own list of the beliefs ingrained in you throughout your childhood.*
   ___
   ___
   ___
   ___

2. *As you study that list now, from this vantage point, be as truthful as you can with yourself to see how self-judgment, doubts and limiting fears have crept into your life.*
   ___
   ___
   ___
   ___

3. *Become aware. How do these beliefs stop you from living fully?*

_____
_____
_____
_____

THROUGH WHAT WE **BELIEVE, THINK & SPEAK** *we are creating and molding* OUR EXPERIENCES.

{ CHAPTER 4 }

***

BUILD IT &
IT WILL COME

1. *Do you feel something stirring inside that is prompting you to change? Are you listening or pushing it away?*

   _____
   _____
   _____
   _____

2. *Knowing you have the capability to have, do or be anyone you choose, assess your life. On a scale of 1 – 10 with ten being super amazing:*

   1 2 3 4 5 6 7 8 9 10 = SUPER AMAZING

   _____
   _____
   _____
   _____

3. *How would you rate your career in terms of satisfaction and fulfillment?*

1 2 3 4 5 6 7 8 9 10 = SUPER AMAZING

_____
_____
_____

4. *How would you rate your personal relationships?*

1 2 3 4 5 6 7 8 9 10 = SUPER AMAZING

_____
_____
_____

5. *How would you rate your level of abundance?*

1 2 3 4 5 6 7 8 9 10 = SUPER AMAZING

_____
_____
_____

6. *Rating your significant other. Is the love of your life meeting your needs?*

1 2 3 4 5 6 7 8 9 10 = SUPER AMAZING

_____
_____
_____

7. *Do you exercise in some form and how do you rate your health?*

1 2 3 4 5 6 7 8 9 10 = SUPER AMAZING

_____
_____
_____

CHAPTER 5

✳ ✳ ✳

The DISCOVERY: WE ARE NOT *Who We* BELIEVE *We Are*

1. *Make a list of your latest Ego identifiers.*

   - _____
   - _____
   - _____
   - _____
   - _____
   - _____
   - _____
   - _____
   - _____
   - _____
   - _____
   - _____
   - _____

2. *As you progress through your life. What are some other ways you have added to your Ego identity? Can you begin to see how they may limit you?*

   _____
   _____
   _____
   _____

3. *Looking at a day, a week or a month in your life. What opportunities are you giving yourself to react to? Be specific.*

   _____
   _____
   _____
   _____

4. *What are the predominant feelings or State of Mind that recur in your life?*

   _____
   _____
   _____
   _____

5. *As you awaken each day, where is your focus? And what experiences in your life tend to remain the same or have not changed?*

   _____
   _____
   _____
   _____

{ CHAPTER 6 }

***

SEEKING
&
ASKING

1. *Your number 1 desire. Start with one situation, person or event. Focusing in this one area, what do you really want to attract/bring into your life experience?*

   _____
   _____
   _____
   _____
   _____

2. *What does your mind, belief or patterning tell you about attracting this into your life?*

   _____
   _____
   _____
   _____
   _____

3. What new statement can you construct that reinforces the belief you can attract and experience what you wish?

_____
_____
_____
_____

4. We all have patterns of thought and behavior. Patterns are a part of life conditioning and a learning process for growth. What pattern of thought or behavior do you have throughout your life that will sabotage your success? How does it show up?

_____
_____
_____
_____

5. Have you been triggered by an event or situation recently? What does the Ego Identity believe about yourself that creates this reaction?

_____
_____
_____
_____

6. What have you learned from life that you can now identify as something you wish to unlearn?

_____
_____
_____
_____

CHAPTER 7

* * *

The BASICS: SCIENCE & SPIRITUALITY

1. Do you have an analytical, scientific way of viewing the world or a spiritual heart centered way of viewing the world?

   _____
   _____
   _____
   _____

2. Can you accept others and their way of walking in this world? Are you able to allow them to be, without judgement? Can you see the advantage of becoming open to changing your viewpoint?

   _____
   _____
   _____
   _____

3. *Identify now how your way of perceiving yourself has limited you in the past. What are some of the old concepts that relate to Science or Spirituality that are not of higher truth?*

_____
_____
_____
_____

4. *Explain the concept of good and bad. Can you begin to understand how all experiences are for our highest good?*

_____
_____
_____
_____

5. *God is not the old man with a beard up there somewhere. Can you understand how God - without judgement - is all love? How Godly are you? Explain how you predominantly see the world.*

_____
_____
_____
_____

6. *Every experience has the capability to mirror back to us what we believe. What mirrors or monkeys are showing up in your life? What pattern or belief are they mirroring to you or showing you?*

_____
_____
_____
_____

CHAPTER 8

***

The
PERSONAL
IDENTITY

1. Write out the major event patterns in your life. What questions/statements do you repeatedly ask/tell yourself when these events take place?

   _____
   _____
   _____
   _____

2. Learn the construct of your mind. Your mind believes your story and makes it true! What story do you identify with? Take a moment, a day or a week to become aware and write down your thoughts regarding the story you continually tell yourself, and the person you have become. Can you see how you came to believe this about yourself?

   _____
   _____
   _____
   _____

WORKBOOK EXCERCISES & ACTIVITIES

3. Becoming aware is key to releasing your addictions. In what ways do you re-affirm your addictive states of mind?

___
___
___
___

4. According to the Enlightened Masters, you chose to come here. You, or your soul wanted this experience and came into this world at a perfect time to learn from the physical and expand your consciousness. What do you believe your soul lesson is? From a soul level, what are the major gifts your life is giving you?

___
___
___
___

5. Can you see why it is so important to understand where you place your focus each day and why changing your focus will change your experience? In observing yourself can you see clearly where your focus is on most days?

___
___
___
___

6. What are the six items that make up your Ego or Separate Self?

___
___
___
___

CHAPTER 9

***

Love THYSELF

1. *Speaking of love. Do you love who you are? Do you love how you look? How you perform? When you have difficulty, can you love yourself and your experience? Can you see the gift in your experience and love your mirrors/monkeys?*

   _____
   _____
   _____
   _____

2. *What event or person is in your life that you are having difficulty excepting? What is your recurring emotional addiction? What is your higher learning or lesson?*

   _____
   _____
   _____
   _____

3. *Read over the Universal Fears. Which of the Universal fears are prevalent in your life? How do these fears present themselves? Bring awareness and identify how the fear shows up, through a person, situation or event.*

_____
_____
_____
_____

4. *Make a list of the people or events who you believe hurt you. This list contains everyone you need to forgive. What were the emotional addictions or beliefs this person, place or event brought to light?*

_____
_____
_____
_____

5. *What are your major lessons learned from these events and interactions? Seeing from a higher perspective, a soul perspective, what was this teaching you? Can you forgive them ..and forgive yourself?*

_____
_____
_____
_____

6. *Walk through the steps to "Loving Yourself." Write out your answers.*

_____
_____
_____
_____

CHAPTER 10

***

DEFINING *Your* END RESULT

1. *What are you, "hanging on to" in your life in order to feel "safe," that really does not feel good or limits you in some way? What are you fearful of? Describe here.*

   _____
   _____
   _____
   _____

2. *Sit in your favorite place. Get quiet, close your eyes and allow your mind to focus on your breathing. Ask yourself, what does your heart really want? Are you ready to bring it into your life?*

   _____
   _____
   _____
   _____

3. Its time to create Heart Based intentions. If you have goals in a particular area of your life, how can you redefine these goals to resonate with you and bring joy as you read them? Create intentions in the following 7 areas of your life:

   Career/Service: _____
   _____

   Relationships/Love: _____
   _____

   Financial/Abundance: _____
   _____

   Personal: _____
   _____

   Health/Fitness: _____
   _____

   Recreation/Fun: _____
   _____

   Legacy/What you leave to the world: _____
   _____

4. Read your intentions again. When you read them out loud, do you feel excitement and joy?

   _____
   _____
   _____
   _____

5. Let's discover your routine as you awaken each day? Where do your thoughts go? What people, place or events are becoming routine? Write here how you can refocus with higher emotion on your End Results! This will later become a meditation for you.

   _____
   _____
   _____
   _____

CHAPTER 11

✱ ✱ ✱

How We SABOTAGE OUR OWN JOY

1. Describe a situation or event in your life where you blame others for your situation.

   What predominant state of mind are you experiencing? _____
   _____

   Who or what is the mirror or monkey? _____
   _____

   What story is your mind making up? _____
   _____

2. How is your experience perfect for you?

   _____
   _____
   _____
   _____

3. What statements can you create to be grateful for this experience?

　
　
　
　

4. In my story of, "You Are A Man Act Like One" I had the experience of pushing away abundance. Find an area of your life where you are sabotaging your ability to live abundantly. Where did your story begin? What is the old belief in the way of your abundance?

　
　
　
　

5. What is the Divine perfection in your story? Are you able to see the blessing in your burden? Can you take ownership of it? What is the hidden obstacle that you can now breakthrough?

　
　
　
　

6. Finding gratitude, to shift your perspective is huge, life changing and healing. Any suffering is the Ego or a Separate Self Identity attachment to an old emotional addiction and the past. Write out how you can be grateful for this experience and prepare to release it.

EPILOGUE

***

Coming HOME

1. *Soul growth. Thinking back, from a young age the mirrors and actors in your play, (your life), have provided opportunities to feel and react in similar ways. What are the predominant states of mind your soul is seeking to learn from?*

   _____
   _____
   _____
   _____

2. *Have your challenges and issues become clear? What are they?*

   _____
   _____
   _____
   _____

3. To become free and fulfilled and "Let Go of The Shit Show" we must become aware, be grateful for our experience and accept healing. The Ego, loves to preserve conflict and preserves it through blaming and projecting on others. When you think of or choose to become powerful, courageous and live from your Divine Essence, what is your Ego Reaction?

_____

_____

_____

_____

4. Meditation is a powerful way to connect with Divine infinite intelligence and become one with all we desire. Bringing ourselves into the present, letting go of neediness, stress and who the Ego believes we are is key in this powerful process. What is the first person, place or event we wish to become one with? Does a visual picture of this in your mind bring joy?

_____

_____

_____

_____

Start a 10 minute meditation process as described in the text. Sit in your favorite place, where you can enjoy peace. Let yourself breathe. Close your eyes. As your mind wanders, which it will, gently bring your focus back to the present moment, and back to focus on your breathing. Cool air coming in through the nose, warm air leaving the mouth. As you meditate, start to feel. Feeling the body. Feeling your breathing. Many of us need to cultivate a connection to our heart and mind. We begin this through feeling. Let peace begin to flow through the mind and body. With time imagine your energy becoming whole, the heart and mind in sync. Feel the amazing energy around you. When you feel ready, imagine your first person or event you wish to become one with. Imagine this in a beautiful setting and feel the joy of this event as if it has become true. Hold the image for several seconds, feel the joy until it's time to let go.

You may focus on any end result or intention and as you increase the time you meditate, allow events, people and synchronicity's to come into your life. Heal yourself. Release doubt. Release fear. Feel the joy of becoming one with it. Continue daily.

Thank you for enjoying this experience with me! I trust that it will serve you well!

LOVE YOUR ADVENTURE!

-Michael

www.ingramcontent.com/pod-product-compliance
Lightning Source LLC
Chambersburg PA
CBHW080416170426
43194CB00015B/2832